THE
GHOSTLY TALES
OF
TOMBSTONE

T0016881

Published by Arcadia Children's Books
A Division of Arcadia Publishing
Charleston, SC
www.arcadiapublishing.com

Spooky America is a trademark of Arcadia Publishing, Inc.

First published 2023

Manufactured in the United States

ISBN 978-1-4671-9735-9

Library of Congress Control Number: 2023931846

All images courtesy of Shutterstock.com; pp. 12-13 1960s Travis/Shutterstock.com;
pp. 30-31 Atomazul/Shutterstock.com; p. 32 evenfh/Shutterstock.com;
pp. 102-103 ehrlif/Shutterstock.com

Notice: The information in this book is true and complete to the best of our
knowledge. It is offered without guarantee on the part of the author or Arcadia
Publishing. The author and Arcadia Publishing disclaim all liability in connection with
the use of this book.

Spooky America

THE
GHOSTLY TALES
OF

TOMBSTONE

ANNA LARDINOIS

Adapted from *Haunted Tombstone* by Cody Polston

arcadia®
CHILDREN'S BOOKS

ARIZONA

TOMBSTONE

TABLE OF CONTENTS & MAP KEY

Welcome to Spooky Tombstone!

They call Tombstone the town too tough to die. If you look at the history of this rowdy Wild West town, you'll probably agree with its reputation. For more than a century, gunslingers, gamblers, outlaws, and thieves mingled with the miners and lawmen who called these dusty streets home.

But with a name like Tombstone, you shouldn't be surprised to learn there are others who call this place home...GHOSTS!! Lots and lots of ghosts. In fact, like most towns with a violent past, more spirits haunt Tombstone's streets than you could possibly imagine. It's known as one of the most *haunted* places in Arizona. But how did all these spooks get here?

The story of Tombstone began when a miner named Ed Schieffelin discovered a massive vein of silver in the San Pedro Valley in 1877. Overnight, Schieffelin became a very wealthy man. He used some of that wealth to expand his mining operation. When he did, he found even more silver! Word of all that silver spread

quickly. Soon, more people started moving into the area to try their own luck at silver mining.

In the blink of an eye, the town grew. In 1877, the area had just a handful of residents, many of them living in tents. By 1885, nearly 10,000 people called Tombstone home!

You might not believe it, but Tombstone was like many other Southwest towns at the time. It had churches and libraries and newspapers. But history does not remember these things. When most people think about Tombstone, they imagine saloons, gambling dens, dancehalls, and of course, shootouts.

There is a good reason for this. Tombstone was a dangerous place from the beginning. The first shipment of precious metal left the mines in summer 1877. By autumn, the first stagecoach robbery occurred.

Tombstone was a tough place, and you had to be tough to survive there. Tempers ran as hot as an Arizona summer. And everybody in town had a gun.

Back then, the lawmen weren't always trustworthy. History remembers the Cochise County sheriff, John Behan, as a corrupt man. People say he used his position to protect criminals and to settle scores with his enemies. Even the lawmen who *are* remembered fondly, like the badge-wearing Earp brothers, weren't always to be trusted. Virgil,

6

Morgan, and Wyatt Earp were all known to bend, and sometimes outright BREAK, the law if it suited them!

Another thing that made life difficult in Tombstone was fire. The desert town did not have much water, and just about everything in town was made of wood. Once a fire started, it was very hard to put it out.

Tombstone's first big fire occurred in 1881. A lit cigar came in contact with a barrel of whiskey at the Arcade Saloon. The blaze quickly moved beyond the saloon and raged until sixty-six businesses were destroyed.

The tough town immediately began to rebuild. But a year later, fire once again devastated Tombstone. In 1882, a blaze started in a downtown laundry. It quickly moved to the Grand Hotel. The flames continued through the city, reducing over one hundred buildings to ash.

Still not ready to give up, the town rebuilt. Then the floods came. In those days, miners dug deep into the earth to find the treasures they sought. Most of the time, they found nothing but rocks. Rarely, they would find the metals that would make them rich—like gold and silver. But on a few occasions, the miners discovered underground beds of water. The water flooded the mines and made it

impossible for the miners to do their job. The only solution was to install pumps in the mines to flush out the water.

This solution worked for a while. But in 1886, a terrible fire destroyed the pumps. The mines flooded, and this time, there was no easy way to clear the water out. The mines closed. Miners moved out of town to find work elsewhere. Tombstone's population dwindled.

But the town continued on. Many townspeople refused to abandon the homes and businesses they had built—and rebuilt. They didn't want to leave. (And some of them never did!)

Today, Tombstone is a favorite destination for people who want a taste of life in the Wild West—*and* who want to meet a ghost or two along the way. You can stroll with the spirits among the shops and saloons of Allen Street. You can watch for ghosts with their guns drawn at the O.K. Corral, the sight of the most famous gunfight in Wild West history. You can test your bravery and head one hundred feet underground to a real—and REALLY spooky—1880's silver mine. You can even ramble with the restless souls at the old Boothill Graveyard, a place that might just have you shaking in *your* boots.

Wherever you roam, be sure to tip your hat to those who call Tombstone home ... people who are a lot like the town itself: too tough to die! (Or, so it seems, by the number of ghosts lurking around these parts.)

Are you tough enough to handle the terrifying tales of Tombstone? Read on, if you dare.

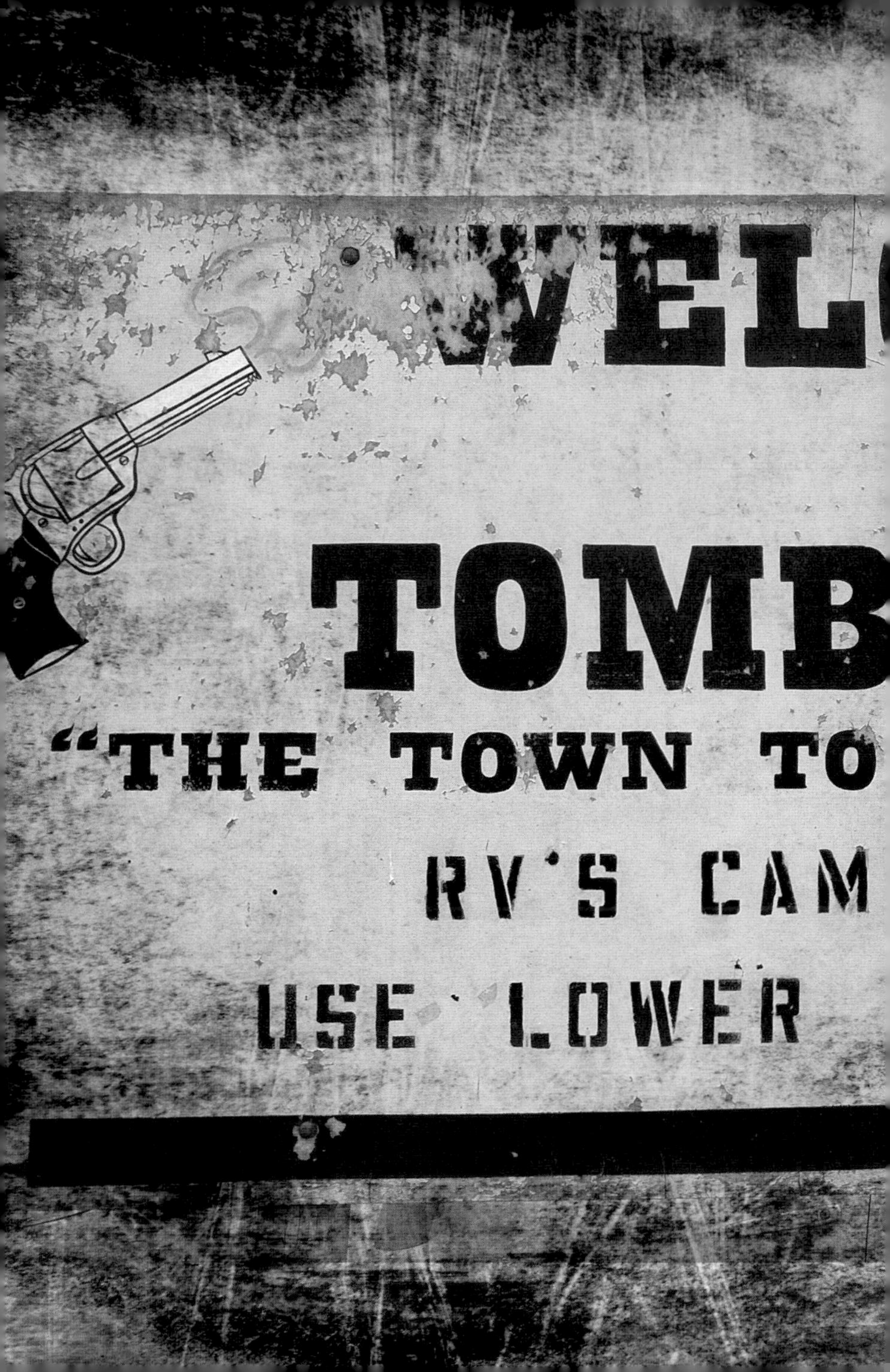
WELC
TOMB
"THE TOWN TO
RV'S CAM
USE LOWER

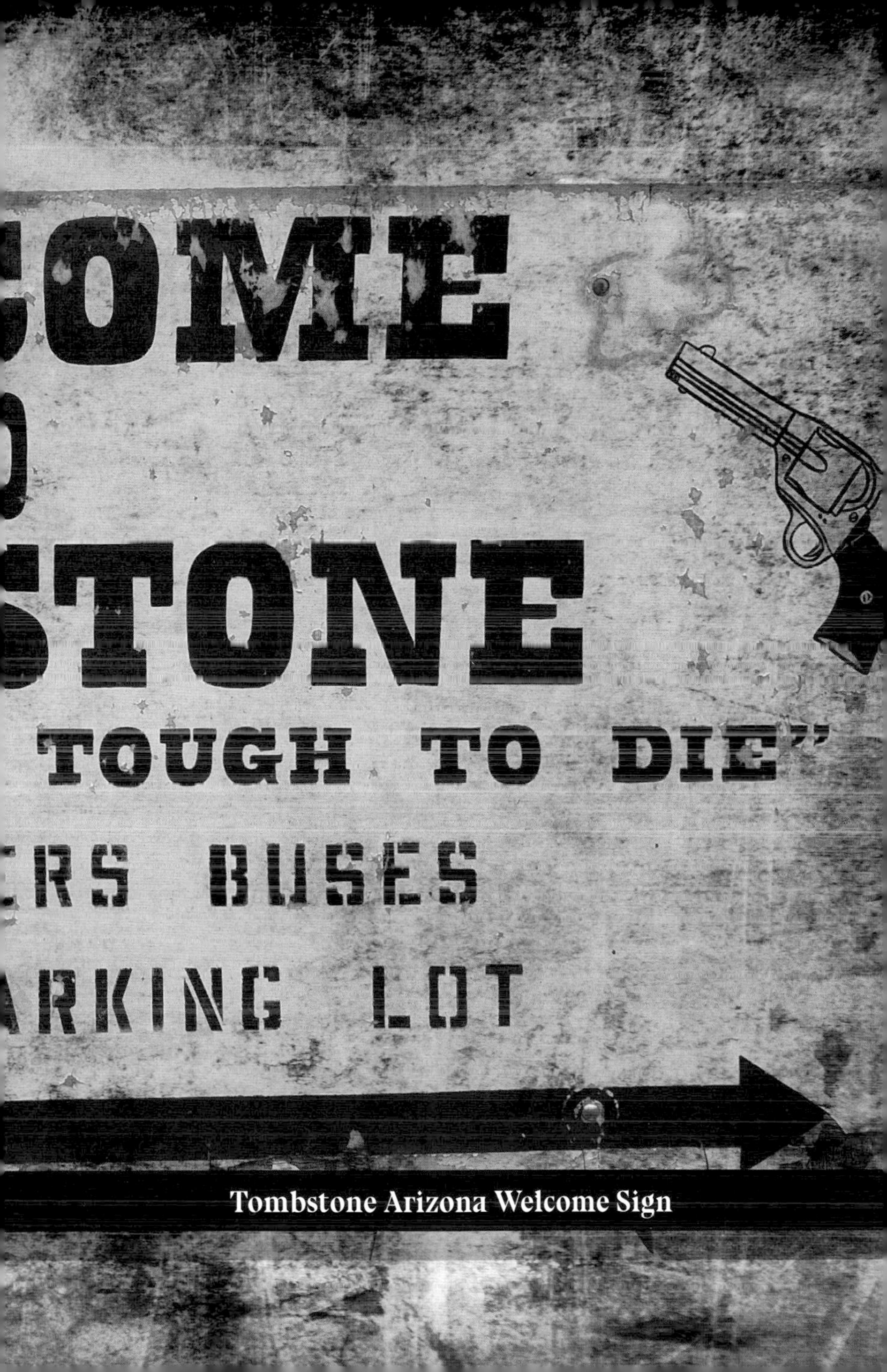

COME
STONE
"TOUGH TO DIE"
RS BUSES
ARKING LOT

Tombstone Arizona Welcome Sign

The Otherworldly Side of the O.K. Corral

You might already know about the most famous gunfight in the Wild West—the shootout at the O.K. Corral. You can see the legendary, thirty-second-long showdown reenacted in countless movies. You can read about it in books. There are even songs about the deadly battle. All over the world, people know about the corral.

But, did you know the location is haunted? It sure is!

The O.K. Corral, or the Old Kindersley Corral, was in business from 1879 until 1888. Most of the people who lived in Tombstone then did not own their own horses. O.K. Corral rented horses and carriages to those who needed them. People who visited Tombstone would bring their horses to the building to be fed and cared for while in town. A business that provides these services is called a livery.

The O.K. Corral is still known today because of what happened a few doors down from the building on the afternoon of October 26, 1881.

In the rural land around Tombstone, there roamed a dangerous gang of men known as the Cowboys. They were cattle rustlers, horse thieves, bandits, and murderers. Back then, the word "cowboy" meant outlaw, and the gang lived up to their reputation.

The roving band of criminals and the Earp family of lawmen had no love for each other.

For years, tensions had been growing between them. On October 25, 1881, Cowboy members Ike Clanton and Tom McLaury came into Tombstone for supplies. The next day, Ike's brother, Billy, rode into town to join the men, along with Frank McLaury and Billy Claiborne. Townspeople were on edge as the gang moved through the town.

Earlier that year, Tombstone enacted a law stating that anyone entering the city limits must surrender their weapons at a livery or saloon as soon as they arrived. This law was not limited to six-shooters (a kind of revolver very popular at the time). Everything from bowie knives and dirks (short daggers), to rifles and pistols needed to be turned in.

The Earps suspected the Cowboys did not follow this law. Wyatt Earp, a lawman and gambler, believed that the outlaws not only had guns but had been filling their cartridge belts with bullets when they visited Spangenberg's gun shop on Fourth Street.

Later that day, people in town heard the five outlaws talking about killing the Earps. That was enough for the lawmen. They decided to confront the Cowboys. The city marshal, Virgil

Earp, gathered his brothers Morgan and Wyatt, and their friend Doc Holliday. Armed and ready for a fight, the men went out in search of the Cowboys.

The Earps and Holliday found the outlaws on a vacant lot on Fremont Street, behind the O.K. Corral.

The rest, as they say, is history. The men confronted each other. Within thirty seconds, thirty bullets were fired in what would become known as the most infamous shootout in the American Old West. When the dust settled, Billy Clanton and Tom and Frank McLaury were dead. Virgil and Morgan Earp and Doc Holliday were wounded. Ike Clanton and Billy Claiborne fled when the bullets began to fly, escaping injury. Wyatt Earp was unhurt.

When the bodies were hauled away, the Cochise

County sheriff, John Behan, arrested the Earp brothers and Doc Holliday for the murder of the three men. The lawmen went to jail, but not for long. A month later, they were released when a Tombstone judge found them not guilty. He believed the men were "fully justified in committing these homicides."

History still remembers the events of October 26, 1881—but not just because it is an exciting story. There are ghostly reminders of the deadly gunfight that continue to linger near the site of the O.K. Corral.

Ghosthunters and tourists alike have reported feeling unexplained cold spots near the location of the gunfight. With a daily average temperature of eighty-six degrees Fahrenheit in Tombstone, cold spots are bound to startle even the bravest ghost enthusiast!

The spirits that remain don't just make themselves felt—they can also be seen. An apparition of a tall, thin man wearing a flat-brimmed hat has been spotted roaming the area. Douglas Clay, a manager at the O.K. Corral, reported seeing a lanky figure walk into the building office. When he entered the room to help the man, the manager was startled to find the office empty. The man in the hat had mysteriously vanished!

But the unknown ghostly man is not alone— Tombstone locals and tourists have sensed (or even seen) a number of otherworldly figures thought to be the restless spirits of Cowboys, eager to continue the battle against the Earps into the afterlife. The spooky spirits are dressed in Old West attire, from boots to brimmed hats. The men are ready for battle. People often see them with their guns drawn.

The specters of the long-dead Cowboys have been known to wander away from the site of the gunfight. Over the years, many have reported seeing the ghostly figure of a young man standing at the corner of Fremont Street and Third Street. Could it be that the spirit lingering on the street corner is that of the slain Billy Clanton?

Unbelievably, the battle between the Cowboys and the lawmen is not the *only* famous gunfight connected to the O.K. Corral. There was another murder nearby. And it has a ghost of its own!

The men who arrived on the frontier to make

their fortunes in Tombstone were a hard lot. Jim Burnett was one of those men. Burnett had a ranch on the San Pedro River. He was also a justice of the peace. The job of the justice of the peace was to resolve disputes and assign punishments when a judge was not available. Burnett could be a ruthless man and had many enemies.

One of his biggest rivals was a fellow rancher named William Cornell Greene. His ranch was also on the San Pedro River and the men were locked in a battle over access to it. Without water, their ranches would fail. But they were unwilling to work together. Both men built dams in the river to supply water to their own ranches, without any consideration for the other.

Burnett wanted to expand his ranch, but he could not do that without more water. Greene's dam made that impossible. So he came up with a sinister plan. Burnett would destroy Greene's dam and take his water.

On the night of June 24, 1897, Burnett had his hired laborers blow up Greene's dam. This decision resulted in the tragic death of two little girls.

Greene's family was unaware the dam had been destroyed. The next morning was a hot one. Greene's daughters Eva and Ella decided to cool off in the river with their friend Katie Corcoran.

The girls often swam in the shallow swimming hole. It was a refreshing way to find relief from the oven-like conditions of

the desert. The girls made their way to the water's edge and Katie jumped in. Instead of landing on her feet in the shallow water as she expected, the girl disappeared under the water.

Ella jumped in next. She immediately knew what was wrong. The water was much, much deeper than it had ever been. The swimming hole was no longer a shallow body of water where the girls could safely play. It was deep. And dangerous.

Struggling to keep her head above water, Ella cried out to her sister.

"Go back! Go back," she warned Eva.

Eva ran home as fast as she could to get help. But by the time she retuned with grown-ups, Katie and Ella had already drowned. They could not keep their heads above the deep water, and they could not reach the shore.

William Greene was devastated over the loss of his daughter and her friend. He knew the dam explosion had caused their deaths. He was enraged and wanted vengeance.

Greene offered a $1,000 reward for anyone who could lead him to who'd blown up his dam. That is about $35,000 in today's money. The reward tempted a laborer who was involved in the destruction of the dam. The man revealed that Burnett was behind the deadly explosion.

With his guns loaded, Greene set out to find John Burnett and make him pay for the deaths of the two girls.

Greene found the man on the streets of Tombstone on July 1. The grieving father caught up with the justice of the peace on Allen Street, near the O.K. Corral. When Greene spotted the man, he called out to him, accusing him of blowing up his dam.

Burnett denied the accusation, but Greene was unconvinced. He aimed his gun at Burnett and pulled the trigger three times. Burnett collapsed in the street and died.

Greene immediately surrendered to the police. The only statement he gave the authorities was, "I have no statement to make other than that man was the cause of my child being drowned." Greene was arrested and tried for the murder, but he was acquitted.

If you believe the tales, Burnett does not rest in peace. Instead, his restless spirit continues to roam the street where he was gunned down.

To this day, locals claim to see his ghost more frequently than any other specters who haunt the area.

Ghostly Burnett is a balding old man who lingers outside the corral. The apparition has a distinct beard heavily peppered with gray hairs. Though he appears often, people who've seen the old man say he disappears without a trace when approached by the living.

What keeps these undead gunslingers tied to the O.K. Corral and the land around it? Does something paranormal tie the spirits to the area? Or do they remain because their lives ended before they were ready to move on?

Most importantly, are you brave enough to approach a ghostly Cowboy—or the sinister Burnett—to try and find out? I know I am not!

The O.K. Corral

BIG NOSE KATE'S

SALOON

SALOON

WE'VE GOT FOOOD!

ATM
INSIDE

BIG NOSE KATE'S
SALOON
FREE WESTERN
ENTERTAINMENT
DAILY

AWARDED

BEST "COWBOY"
BAR IN THE
WEST

The Spooktacular Big Nose Kate's Saloon

Long before it was Big Nose Kate's Saloon, the building at 417 E. Allen Street was the Grand Hotel. It was said to be the most elegant hotel in all of Arizona when it opened its doors in 1880.

Everyone with enough money in their pockets stayed at the Grand. Famous lawmen Virgil and Wyatt Earp and their friend Doc Holliday spent many nights in the posh hotel.

The Grand was also popular with outlaws. Cowboy gang members Ike Clayton and the McLaury brothers were guests at the hotel, too.

Sadly, the hotel burned down during the fire of 1882. When firefighters finally doused the flames, only the frame of the building remained. Townspeople rebuilt the structure, but it was never a luxurious hotel again. It's now a popular tourist attraction. The saloon is named for Mary Katherine Horony Cummings, who is much better known as Big Nose Kate. I'll let you guess how she got that nickname. She is one of the most well-known pioneering women in the Wild West.

The lady with the oversized schnoz is remembered in history as an outlaw, and as the longtime girlfriend of Doc Holliday. They were a hard-drinking pair who loved to gamble and fought like cats and dogs. Kate's life story is *almost* as wild as the history of the city she once called home!

Now that you know the story behind the building and its name, let's get into the good stuff ghosts!

The otherworldly entities in the building first made themselves known when the owners decided to create a gift shop in the basement. Shortly after construction began, the employees in the saloon started hearing strange noises coming from the dark corners of the underground room.

One night after the saloon closed, some of the employees were sitting on the basement steps chatting. Someone heard the odd noise again and motioned the others to be quiet. In the silence, they all heard it. It was the sound of footsteps coming toward them from the unlit basement!

The sound startled the workers because they did not think anyone was in the basement. One of them flicked on a flashlight and pointed it in the direction of the sound. The light beam lit up the basement. But no one was there. At least, that is what they thought at the time.

Puzzled, and yet relieved, the workers started chatting again. They'd almost forgotten the incident, until they heard *another* sound that stopped them all in mid-sentence. It was

a loud, terrible moan. Everyone heard it. It sounded like someone in pain. Their hearts beat faster as they stared at one another, wondering what to do.

With a slightly shaking hand, the employee with the flashlight turned it on again. From the stairs, the group scanned the basement, but once again, they found nothing hiding in the dark. At least nothing they could see. With the eerie sense that they were not alone in the basement, despite what their eyes were telling them, the group headed back upstairs.

But that was not the last time paranormal activity was detected in the basement.

The construction crew discovered something unexpected. It was a small room that had once been the living quarters of the janitor who worked at the Grand Hotel.

As they started to tear down the room, they found a secret panel like a hatch door in the middle of the room's floor. When they slid the panel open, they uncovered a secret tunnel. The tunnel led to the maze of underground mine tunnels under the streets of Tombstone.

A few brave employees grabbed some flashlights and lowered themselves into the hole to investigate. They discovered the secret tunnel led to one of the Toughnut mine shafts. Satisfied, they headed back to the saloon.

One by one, the employees pulled themselves up out of the hole in the ground and back into the small basement room. When the last of the group emerged from the hole, they heard a bone-chilling sound!

A deep moan echoed down the basement steps toward the small room with the secret tunnel. The employees froze. Then they heard a rush of footsteps thundering down the staircase.

The hair stood up on the backs of their necks. The owner of the building was *certain* all the doors were locked. No one else could possibly be in the saloon. Maybe there were other ways to enter the saloon that they didn't know about? Or maybe they had just heard a ghost!

Armed with nothing more than flashlights, the group explored the basement looking for the source of the sound. They checked each corner and searched behind every door. No one was there.

They courageously climbed the basement stairs and began to search the saloon. Every door and window in the building was locked. They searched every room and checked every closet. But still, they found no one.

If there wasn't anyone else in the building, who had been moaning and running down the basement stairs?

Many think what they heard was The Swamper. Back in the 1880s, janitors were known as swampers. The old janitor of the Grand Hotel lived in the small basement room. It is assumed he created the hidden tunnel underneath the floor of his bedroom, likely to gain access to the silver mine and steal the precious metal.

Here is where the legend comes in.

Some people say the miners discovered that the old janitor was stealing from them. When the angry men confronted the thief, he fell—or was thrown—down the flight of basement stairs, where he died. It is said the otherworldly sounds in the basement are The Swamper reliving his final, terrible moments.

But others disagree. They think the janitor got away with stealing from the mines but never had the chance to sell his stolen silver. They claim his stash is still hidden somewhere in the basement. And that the ghost of the old swamper makes noise to try and frighten people out of the basement—and away from his secret stash of precious silver.

No one knows for certain if it is the ghostly swamper whose spirit still lingers in the basement. But this mysterious basement-dwelling spirit is not the only one that haunts Big Nose Kate's Saloon. In the same way construction can rustle up rats and other critters, the work in the building seems to have awoken a great deal of paranormal activity.

Employees report hearing people talking and singing in empty rooms. Doors inside the saloon open and close, seemingly on their own. Lights turn themselves on and off without warning. Disembodied footsteps have been reported throughout the building.

There is one unseen spirit who seems to have made itself right at home in the saloon—a spirit, or even a mischievous poltergeist, that demands to be noticed. The wait staff have named this entity Felix.

Felix does not keep his hands to himself. He is known to touch the servers. He will occasionally pinch them, hit them, or pull their hair. The contact is not painful, but it is startling. Imagine standing in the middle of a room by yourself and then suddenly feel a lock of your hair being yanked!

The unseen specter can make the glasses on the wait staff's serving trays levitate (float in the air). Once the glasses are hovering above the tray, this mischievous spirit will throw the drinks in the employee's face or on their chests! Needless to say, Felix is not popular with the staff.

Not all the ghosts in Kate's Saloon are unseen, however. One night, an employee was closing the saloon for the evening. He made a final walk around the building to make sure the doors were locked and everything was ready for business the next day. As he walked by the bar, he noticed someone leaning on it. It was a man in a long duster coat, just like the ones that cowboys used to wear.

The employee started to let the man know the saloon was closed. He turned for a moment to put away some glasses, but when he looked back, there was no one at the bar. Or anywhere else. The employee froze. The cowboy was nowhere to be found. He had completely disappeared!

Terrified, the employee ran out of the saloon and called his manager from across the street. He told the manager, "You can go lock up Big Nose Kate's. I'm not going back over there." And he never did. It was the very last time the frightened man ever stepped foot inside the saloon.

That is not the only unnerving thing that has happened after the saloon was closed for the night.

Tim "Whiskers" Ferrick came to Big Nose Kate's after closing time to interview for a job. Tim and his wife, Marcy, sat at the corner table of the saloon with the owner and talked about the job. During their conversation, Tim asked the owner about the saloon's reputation as a haunted building.

The owner had started to tell Tim and Marcy about the haunted tunnel in the basement when a loud scraping sound interrupted him. It was coming from above where they were sitting. The trio looked up and noticed something moving on the decorative balcony above the dining room.

The balcony is there to give saloon visitors the feeling they are still in the Old West. Two mannequins are displayed on the balcony, one man and one woman. Both of the statues are dressed in clothing that was popular when Tombstone was a boom town.

To their shock, the female mannequin began swaying. It slowly moved forward, and then, as if being pushed by someone or something unseen, hit the balcony railing with such force that it flipped over. It fell to the dining room floor with a crash that echoed through the empty building.

The group sat in stunned silence. What in the world had just happened? No one was anywhere near the mannequins or the balcony. How had the mannequin, as big as a real person, flipped over a railing all by *itself*?

But this strange scene was far from over!

Tim looked back at the balcony, trying to

understand what had just happened. That's when he saw something that sent a shiver up his spine.

Shaking, he pointed to the balcony and cried, "Hey! Look at the other mannequin!"

They all looked up and watched in disbelief as the male mannequin began to move. Slowly, it turned its head toward the empty space where the female mannequin had been just moments before. Seeing such a thing with their own eyes was all it took. The trio decided they had enough ghost talk for the night and quickly left the saloon.

With all the paranormal activity this building has had, it's no wonder ghost hunters frequently stop in to investigate the reports of otherworldly events.

 Paranormal investigator Cody Polston witnessed a startling

event when he was in the saloon to conduct an investigation.

After finishing an examination of the building, Cody sat at the bar talking with the bartender on duty. But their friendly conversation didn't last long. Suddenly—from the opposite end of the otherwise empty bar—an unexplained sound interrupted them. It was the ringing sound of a glass vibrating.

Cody and the bartender looked to see what was making the sound. The answer was astonishing! Both men saw a glass beer mug levitate off the bar. As they watched, dumbfounded, the empty mug hung in the air about twelve inches off the surface of the bar. Then, without warning, the glass sailed across the room! It shattered as it fell to the floor.

Cody was shocked, but the bartender wasn't. Instead, the man walked behind the bar, quietly got out a notepad, and began to write notes. The shocked ghost hunter asked the bartender what he was doing. He calmly replied, "We have to keep track of the ones that get broken by the ghosts."

The paranormal investigator left the saloon certain that the reports of supernatural activity in the building were true. But two big questions remained: Who are the spirits that haunt Big Nose Kate's saloon? And *why* are they there?

To this day, no one knows. But there is one thing *nobody* questions: Big Nose Kate's Saloon is one of the most haunted places in all of Tombstone.

Tombstone's Finest: The Crystal Palace Saloon

In a town that had over one hundred saloons, the Crystal Palace stood out. Some townsfolk were still living in tents and crude adobe shelters (adobe is a kind of building material made from sun-dried clay and straw) at the time. But the luxurious Crystal Palace had an indoor fountain that sparkled with brilliant orange goldfish swimming through its water.

In fact, in the whole Arizona Territory, there was nowhere finer than the Crystal Palace. The saloon served the best drinks. It had the best singers and entertainers on staff. And all the gambling in the building was honest—a rarity in those days, when cheating was quite common. The owners worked hard to run a clean establishment, which meant keeping Tombstone's rowdiest residents away from the saloon.

But that wasn't always easy. Especially since everybody who was *anybody* came to the Palace. Virgil Earp, who was both Deputy U.S. Marshal and the Tombstone City Marshal, worked there. Doc Holliday and Big Nose Kate often met at the Crystal Palace for drinks. Night after night, their friends the Earp brothers joined them, along with just about everyone else whose names are part of Tombstone history.

Even though it had a classy reputation, things at the Palace could still sometimes get rowdy. (This *was* the old Wild West, after all.) Fights and brawls occasionally broke out. There were arguments, shootouts, and attempted robberies. Sometimes Mother Nature got rowdy, too! Over the years, the Crystal Palace faced fires, floods, and even an earthquake. It's said the crystal chandeliers shook, swung, and crashed to the floor.

Somehow, through all of that, the Crystal Palace kept its doors open. It stayed open through Prohibition, a time in U.S. history when it was illegal to make or sell liquor. Perhaps, just like Tombstone, the saloon is simply too tough to die.

Today, the saloon remains a favorite of locals and tourists alike. It is also popular with ghost hunters. That's because—you guessed it—it's VERY haunted! Some tourists even believe they have taken home *proof* of paranormal presence in the saloon. While looking over their vacation photos, visitors have spotted unexplained mists and glowing orbs that had not been visible when the photo was taken. Some of the photos have even captured wispy figures that visitors are *certain* look like famous residents from Tombstone's wild past.

According to locals, there are several ghostly "regulars" at the saloon. One is an older man wearing clothing that was in style in the 1880s. Visitors to the saloon often mistake the man for an actor or a tour guide showing off Tombstone's Wild West attractions. The man is sometimes spotted sitting at a table in the saloon. Other times, he can be found sitting at the bar. At some point, the man always stands up and begins to walk to the restroom. After he walks through the doorway, he just disappears!

But just because you can't always see him doesn't mean he's not there. Even invisible, people report feeling his spirit inhabiting the room. Inside the bathroom, the water faucets have been known to turn on and off, seemingly on their own. The lights also seem to operate all by themselves—or by an unseen hand. Toilets flush in empty stalls, scaring people silly. All of this points to paranormal activity. Whether it's the work of the old man's spirit or some other ghostly mischief-maker, something strange—not to mention spooky—is definitely going on here.

Another apparition often mistaken for a Wild West reenactor is that of a pretty young woman dressed in what appears to be a saloon girl costume.

Saloon girls wore fancy dresses with brightly colored ruffled skirts and petticoats that caught the eyes of audience members as they danced. The dresses were often tied near the hip. This would lift the dress and expose the girl's stocking-clad legs. It was a daring look during a time when most women did not even reveal their ankles! With the skirt of the dress hiked up, the saloon girl was able to perform the can-can, a high-energy dance that included high kicks.

The ghostly young woman at the Crystal Palace has been seen wearing a bright red dress with black lace details and black stockings. Her long blonde hair is piled high on top of her head. The elaborate hairdo is topped with a single red feather. It is an outfit worn to attract attention. And the young woman never fails to draw the gaze of everyone in the room. At least . . . those who can see her.

A man named Jeff tells the story of walking into the saloon with his friends while visiting Tombstone. He spotted the woman in red. She was standing alone, near the front door. Her eyes stared out into the saloon, as if she were looking for someone in the crowd.

Jeff admired the woman and decided to ask her to join him at his table. He summoned the courage to approach her. He walked toward her but could not catch the woman's eye. Soon, he was standing right next to her, but she still did not look his way.

He introduced himself and invited the woman to join him, but her eyes remained fixed on the dining room. He continued to talk to her but did not get a response. Then he heard a group of men laughing at a nearby table.

Jeff turned toward the laughter. The men were laughing at him! They asked him who he was talking to and why he was standing alone facing the wall.

Confused, Jeff looked back to the woman in red. But when he turned his head, she wasn't there! It is as if she disappeared into thin air! Startled, Jeff hurried back to his table.

To his relief, the friends seated at his table weren't laughing. They looked just as shocked and frightened as Jeff was. Everyone at the table had seen the pretty woman. They all watched Jeff talk to her. And they all saw her vanish into thin air as Jeff turned his head toward the table of laughing men.

A chill ran over the group of friends. They were certain they had just seen a ghost! They rushed out the door—far away from the Crystal Palace and its supernatural residents!

While the spirit of the older man and saloon girl ghost are the two apparitions most often seen at the Crystal Palace, they are not the only otherworldly characters hanging around. Thirsty cowboys have been known to order drinks at the bar, only to disappear when the bartender turns to make the drink. Doors slam. Empty floors echo with the sound of boots and spurs. Objects move around the room as if by unseen hands. And sometimes, instead of disappearing, a man will *reappear* on another stool across the bar or at a table in the room.

If you're still not convinced ghosts are real, just keep your eye on the old-fashioned roulette wheel hanging on the wall. Once a popular gambling game at the Crystal Palace, the roulette wheel is now for display *only*—and hangs out of reach of guests and employees. But that doesn't mean it isn't used! In fact, it is not unusual for the wheel to spin seemingly on its own. Perhaps the Palace's ghostly cowboys are still trying their luck at gambling . . . even though their game ended many years ago?

If you see a shadowy cowboy bellied up

to the bar, there is no need to quake in your boots. Simply tip your hat and raise your glass of sarsaparilla (a soft drink similar to root beer) in his direction. If you don't bother that cowpoke, he won't bother you. At least, that's what I've heard.

On second thought, you might just want to steer clear of anyone wearing old-time Western clothing. You never know just who, or *what*, you're talking with!

Morgan Earp's Final Stand?

Have you ever wished you could meet the legendary lawman, Morgan Earp?

If you head over to the Red Buffalo Trading Company in downtown Tombstone, you just might have the chance—that is, if you don't mind meeting a ghost!

Today, the Red Buffalo Trading Company is a store that sells Tombstone souvenirs. But in Earp's day, it was a boisterous place filled with rowdy gunslingers. Back then, it was known as Campbell & Hatch Saloon and Billiard Parlor. It opened in 1880.

Morgan Earp spent his last moments among the living in this building.

It was the night of March 18, 1882. Earp was playing billiards with his friend and co-owner of the saloon, Bob Hatch. The crowd inside the saloon watched the men play. It was a typical night in Tombstone, until 10:50 that evening.

At that moment, a single shot rang out. The bullet came from outside of the saloon. The shooter was standing outside of a glass door at the rear of the room. He raised his gun and fired the weapon through the door.

Shattered glass flew throughout the room as the bullet sped toward Morgan Earp. He was struck on the right side of his stomach. The bullet went straight through him. It shattered his spinal column, then flew out the left side of his body.

But the bullet didn't end its deadly journey there.

After the bullet left Morgan Earp's body, it crossed the room and struck George Berry in the thigh! A second bullet was fired into the room and landed in the wall—just above where the famous Wyatt Earp sat watching his brother play billiards.

When his brother crumpled to the ground, Wyatt leapt to his feet and dragged Morgan away from the window to protect him from additional gunfire.

No more shots were fired that night. The gunman fled, but the damage was already done. Morgan lay on the floor in a seeping pool of his own blood. George Barry was in pain. The bullet was lodged in his thigh and the wound oozed blood.

George would survive his wounds. Morgan would not be as lucky.

Doctors quickly arrived at the saloon, but there was nothing they could do for Morgan. They made the dying man as comfortable as they could on the lounge in the card room of the saloon.

Before long, Virgil, James, and Warren Earp joined their brother Wyatt in the card room to say goodbye to Morgan. Family and friends surrounded the wounded lawman until he took his final breath. He died within an hour of being shot.

Morgan's wife came to collect her husband's body and took him to California, where he was buried. While Morgan's body might have left Tombstone, many people believe his spirit lingers in the place where he was murdered.

The original building where Morgan met his fate burned down in 1882 but was quickly rebuilt. Today, it houses the Red Buffalo Trading Company.

A number of startled witnesses claim to have seen the ghostly figure of Morgan Earp lurking in the back corner of the building, near the place he died. Sometimes, visitors and employees hear boots thudding across the floorboards in otherwise empty rooms. Some employees think Morgan watches over the store, pacing back and forth as he guards the building from gunfire.

Late at night, after everyone has left for the day, an unseen figure tidies up the store. This ghost is so helpful, he has even been known to restock shelves. (Unfortunately, the spirit often puts things on the *wrong* shelves, so the store's living employees end up spending their workdays looking for items the ghost moved the night before.)

If this haunting seems hard to believe, hold on to your cowboy hat! There just might be photographic proof that ghosts linger at the Red Buffalo Trading Company. Years ago, a local photographer, James Kidd, filmed the inside of the building to show the insurance company how the building looked. When he reviewed the footage, he noticed something strange in the place where Morgan was shot.

Kidd stopped the film to take a closer look and received a shock. In a single frame of film, he'd captured not one—but *three*—ghostly figures! Figures who had been COMPLETELY invisible when he'd taken the picture!

The blurry image shows two women and one man. They are all wearing clothing that would have been popular when Tombstone was a bustling town. One of the women appears to be wearing a large hat. The man wears an old-fashioned button-up coat and looks to have long sideburns on his cheeks.

Could the photographer have captured the ghost of Morgan Earp? This single frame of film has been lost, so no one knows for sure. But for those who've experienced strange happenings inside the Red Buffalo Trading Company— from shadowy figures, to eerie footsteps, to unexpected items sitting on shelves—this is all the proof they need to believe Morgan's spirit lives on.

Arizona's Bloodiest Cabin: The Brunckow Cabin

On Charleston Road, between Tombstone and Sierra Vista, sits a house of horrors. Known as the bloodiest cabin in all of Arizona, the old Brunckow Cabin is the site of at least twenty-one murders. Eerily, some of those corpses still remain buried on the blood-stained land.

The cabin was built by Frederick Brunckow. He was a German immigrant who went to college to learn about mining in his native land. After he graduated, Brunckow came to the United States. He used his knowledge of mines to land a job with the Sonora Exploring and Mining Company. Not long after Brunckow was hired, he found silver in a mine near Tombstone.

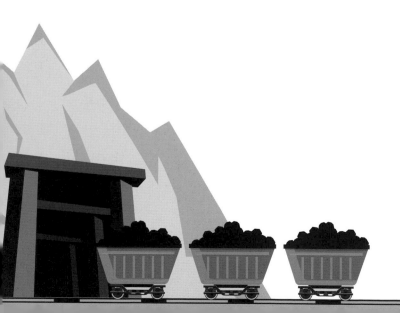

After discovering the silver, workers arrived to help extract it from the mine. Soon buildings began to pop up to meet the needs of the newcomers. Everyone was excited about the silver and hoped the discovery would make them rich beyond their wildest dreams.

One of the men living in the community was William Williams. He and his cousin James, who was a mining engineer, were partners in the mine. On a hot day in July 1860, William saddled his horse and set out to make the thirty-five-mile journey to the town of Fort Buchanan. He went to get a wagonload of flour and planned to return to the mine in a few days.

Four men, including Brunckow, remained near the mine, along with the men they'd hired to work with them. Three days later, William returned to the mine. He was with two boys he'd hired to return the wagon and the horses that carried the flour.

By the time William and the boys arrived, it was after midnight. Right away, William felt uneasy. Though it was late, he sensed an eerie silence along the road. He saw no one and found it strange that the *clip clop* of their horses' hooves hadn't woken a soul. A sinking feeling settled in his stomach when he realized, too, that he did not hear any dogs barking. The dogs that lived near the mine *always* barked when anyone approached the area. Why weren't they barking now?

William began to worry that something was terribly wrong. When he arrived at the mine's small general store, he cautiously dismounted

his horse, fearing what he might find inside. When he walked through the door, the air felt thick and heavy. It was too dark for him to see anything. So, he lit a match to illuminate the room.

What he found was horrifying. Inside the general store, William saw a gruesome scene. Just beyond the doorway lay the body of his cousin, James. Dried blood crusted around the bullet wounds in his lifeless body.

When William was finally able to pull his eyes away from his dead cousin, he realized the store was in shambles. It looked as if there had been a robbery. Most of the store's items had been stolen. What was left behind was broken and tossed around the room.

Panic rose in William's throat. He wondered if whoever had done these terrible things was still nearby. Maybe the murderer was watching him at that very moment!

Full of fear, William quickly gathered up the boys and raced back to Fort Buchanan for help. When they arrived, they told the fort's commander of the gruesome scene they had found. The commander sent troopers to the mine while William and the boys waited and worried.

While the troops were on their way to the mine, a battered and bloody man appeared at the gates of nearby Camp Jecker. The man was David Bontrager. He was the cook for the miners at the same community where William and his cousin lived. The men of Camp Jecker

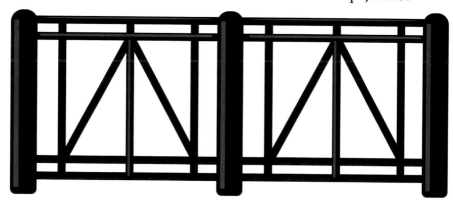

could not have imagined what they were about to hear. David told them there had been a massacre at the mine—and that he was the *only* survivor.

According to David, just hours after William left for Fort Buchanan, two of the mine workers had come into his kitchen and asked for a match to light their cigars. As David turned to grab a match, he heard an explosion of gun shots outside. Within moments, David said, dogs were howling and men were crying out in terror. David ran for the door to see what was happening, but his path was blocked. The two miners in the kitchen would not let him near the doorway.

The miners told David he was now their prisoner. They assured David they would not hurt him because they all followed the same religion. The miners gathered all the merchandise they could take from the store, all the camp's horses and mules, and David, then set out on the road to Sonora, Mexico.

As they led David out of the kitchen, he saw the corpses of the men the miners had killed.

He walked by the bullet-riddled body of James Williams. Morse, another man from the mine, had been shot as well. His blood-splattered body was sprawled on the ground outside of the store. Brunckow was also dead. He had been viciously stabbed to death inside the mine.

The miners marched David out of the make-shift town. His captors held him prisoner until they reached the Mexican border, where they released him. The men of Camp Jecker listened to this terrible story and knew they needed to help. They took David to Fort Buchanan where an investigation of the incident at the mine was already underway.

Not everyone who heard the cook's story

believed him. Some people thought David was not a victim of the miners—but rather, that he had helped them commit the terrible crimes. The commander decided to keep David confined to the guardhouse at the fort. If the troops managed to capture the murderers, David would be right there to identify them. If, on the other hand, David was *part* of this murderous group, they wouldn't have to go far to arrest him.

Meanwhile, the troops from Fort Buchanan arrived at the mine and stepped into a grisly scene. The men found everything David described. They discovered the store, ransacked and looted, as well as the empty animal pens. And sadly, they saw the bodies of the slain men.

But things at the mine had only gotten worse. The dead had been rotting in the hot Arizona sun for days. The smell of decomposing corpses had attracted wolves to the mining camp, and they had feasted upon the fallen men. By the time the troopers came upon the bodies, there was little left of them. In the end, the troops were only able to identify the men by the discarded clothing found near what remained of the bodies.

The smell coming from the bodies revolted the troops, but they did their duty. A soldier at the scene, Sergeant Henderson, later reported, "It made us all sick, but with the help of whiskey and camphor (a kind of oil with a very strong smell) we gave the deceased a good burial."

Ultimately, people came to see that David the cook had told the truth about that terrible day. But no one was ever caught or punished for the massacre at the mine.

The bodies of James, Frederick, and Morse were buried near the Brunckow Cabin. They were the first to be buried there, but not the last.

The mine remained abandoned from that grim day in 1860 until October 23, 1873, when a man named Milton B. Duffield purchased the mine and the surrounding property.

Duffield, who was the first U.S. marshal appointed to the Arizona Territory, wanted to move into the Brunckow Cabin. The problem was, someone was already living there.

A man named James T. Holmes *also* claimed to have purchased the mine and had taken up residence in the cabin. Duffield arrived on June 5, 1874, to run him off the land.

Duffield was a man with a nasty reputation. Everyone knew who he was, but not many liked him. When Holmes saw Duffield approach the cabin, he prepared for violence. Duffield had a hot temper and rushed up to the cabin in a fury. Holmes assumed the marshal was armed, so he grabbed his own double-barreled shotgun. Holmes flung the cabin's front door wide open and, without a moment's hesitation, raised his gun and shot the raging Duffield. To his surprise, when Holmes peered over Duffield's bleeding body, he noticed that the marshal was unarmed.

Duffield's death may have been unjust,

but few shed tears for the fallen lawman. The local newspaper, the *Tucson Citizen,* published an article that announced the man's death. The article said, "He has frequently marched through the streets like an insane person, threatening violence to all who offended him. It is claimed by some men that Duffield had redeeming qualities, but we confess we could never find them."

Holmes was found guilty of the murder and sentenced to three years in prison for the crime. But he never served a single day of his sentence. He escaped custody and fled from the Arizona Territory. He was never seen again.

Duffield was buried near the Brunckow Cabin in an unmarked grave. His body joined those of the three men massacred in 1860.

The seemingly cursed cabin found a new occupant in 1877. Ed Schieffelin, the man who founded Tombstone, used the cabin when he began exploring the area for silver. A few months later, Ed found a massive lode of silver! He escaped the cabin's curse, but others weren't so lucky . . .

In 1897, a gang of bandits were using the remote cabin as a hideout. The five men successfully stole a gold shipment from Wells Fargo. The gang laid low in the cabin, avoiding everyone until interest in the heist died down. They might have gotten away with the crime. But instead, the bandits turned on each other.

No one knows what happened for certain, but it is assumed the men fought about how to split up the stolen gold. The fight turned deadly when the bandits turned their guns on each other.

Later, the bodies of all five men were found in the Brunckow Cabin. Each outlaw had been shot and died from the gunshot wounds. The gold was still in the cabin, untouched.

The gold was returned to Wells Fargo (the very same Wells Fargo banking company that exists today), and the bodies of the five men were buried near the cabin.

After that, the abandoned cabin continued to draw visitors, with deadly results. Tales began to swirl about a man and his son who camped near the cabin, only to be found dead days later. People remembered a prospector who went by himself to explore the abandoned mine. He was later found near the cabin, dead—a single bullet lodged in his back. Later, a family of four was found massacred inside the cabin.

With so much blood spilled on the land, people began to believe something paranormal was causing the many murders that occurred near the Brunckow Cabin.

In 1897, the newspaper the *Tombstone Epitaph* ran a story about what they called a "menacing ghost" that seemed to haunt the land surrounding the notorious Brunckow Cabin. The article claimed that every night an otherworldly being lurked around the dilapidated old cabin. Those who were brave enough to approach the spirit discovered it would vanish the moment they attempted to speak to it.

Within seconds of the ghost's disappearance, however, it would reappear elsewhere on the property. Like a ghostly game of hide-and-seek, it would do this over and over again, eluding the curious humans who tried to make contact.

Not only did people report an active spirit on the land, but they also claimed to hear something coming from the abandoned mine. As people walked near the entrance of the mine, they would hear the clamor of an active worksite coming from inside the shaft. Witnesses said they could hear "pounding on drills, pickaxes pulling away rocks, and the sawing of lumber for trusses."

One newspaper, the *Tombstone Prospector*, reported that some in the community were making plans to investigate the supposedly haunted site.

In time, after so many had died, more and more people across the territory began to believe the land was haunted. In 1881, the *Arizona Democrat* newspaper reported of the Brunckow cabin: "The graves lie thick around the old adobe house." The newspaper went on to add that "prospectors and miners avoid the spot as they would the plague." When asked why, the men claimed that those who had lost their lives on the land still roamed the property.

The stories of ghosts on the property are not a thing of the past. Today, people *still* believe ghosts haunt the bloody Brunckow Cabin.

A group of ghost hunters called Donovan's Ghost Patrol conducted a well-documented investigation of the site in 2017. The investigators roamed the property late into the night using audio equipment to capture paranormal activity. During the examination of the site, several investigators reported hearing the distinct sounds of footsteps moving toward the team.

A scan of the area showed that there were no other humans or animals in the area that could have been the source of the footsteps.

In fact, the investigators were the only living beings on the property. (*Living* being the key word.) But as for the undead? Who can say?

Maybe all those restless souls who lost their lives long ago on the blood-stained land still linger near the Bruckow Cabin. Hundreds of years of ghost stories can't be wrong ... can they?

CHAPTER 6

The Haunts of Boothill Graveyard

Have you heard that old joke about cemeteries? It goes like this:

Why do cemeteries have fences around them? Because people are DYING to get in!

Funny joke, but what if the real reason is a whole lot spookier than that? What if cemeteries have fences because the dead are longing to get OUT...and they need to be...*contained*? That might be the case with Tombstone's oldest cemetery, Boothill Graveyard, where there have been countless reports of paranormal activity over the years. (Talk about a lively afterlife!)

Named for cowboys "buried with their boots on," Boothill is the final resting place for some of Tombstone's finest. To this day, tourists flock to the old cemetery to see the graves of infamous outlaws, gun-slinging gangsters, feisty fugitives, and other Wild West history-makers. The Cowboys who were gunned down at the O.K. Corral—brothers Tom and Frank McLaury and Billy Clanton—are

three of the estimated two hundred and fifty graves inside the Boothill Graveyard.

But the painted wooden grave markers that line this parched patch of desert aren't the only remnants of these colorful characters. Visitors have seen strange lights shining through the dark desert nights from the old boneyard. Sounds that don't come from any human or animal have been reported in the area. Witnesses have claimed to see misty figures rising from the sunbaked earth over the graves of those long dead.

Perhaps *most* chilling are the shadowy human-shaped figures that have been reported

wandering the graveyard at night. It seems as if the dead refuse to rest on this plot of dry, rocky earth that was once the outskirts of town.

Tombstone stopped burying its dead in the Boothill Graveyard in 1883, with a few exceptions. One of those exceptions might be one of the most famous apparitions.

Townsfolk called her China Mary (during this era, when Asian immigrants faced extreme discrimination, Chinese men were often called "John" and women were called "Mary"), but her married name was Mrs. Ah Lum. She was born in China and made her way to the Arizona Territory, where she earned her living as the manager of a well-known general store. Mary was a very popular and well-respected Tombstone resident, known for her good taste and business savvy. When she died in 1906 of heart failure, the whole town came to pay their last respects. They fondly remembered the woman and then laid her to rest in the Boothill Graveyard.

But while her bones may be buried, some believe her spirit remains active—and very much *above* the ground! Many visitors have reported seeing the ghostly figure of an Asian woman wearing a brilliant red dress inside the cemetery gate. Some people think that this often-seen apparition is the spirit of China Mary.

One tourist known to be sensitive to spirits had an encounter with the specter that she'll never forget.

Linda arrived to tour the graveyard before it was open. As she waited to go inside the gates, she spotted a woman walking between the grave markers. The woman's red dress was eye-catching against the brown and dusty desert landscape.

When it was time for the cemetery to open, Linda went inside the visitor's center. The moment she walked through the door, she felt dizzy. She paused for a moment to let the swirling inside her head calm itself. Then she walked toward the woman behind the counter.

Linda was curious to know what the woman in the red dress was doing inside the cemetery. She assumed the woman was an employee of Boothill Graveyard. So, Linda asked the woman behind the counter about the woman she had spotted earlier.

The woman behind the counter gave Linda

a puzzled look. She told Linda she was the only one working there that day. She added that no one should be inside the cemetery.

Linda was *positive* she had seen a woman in a red dress inside the graveyard gates. Now, she was even more curious! But without any more information, all she could do was take a map of the graveyard and head outside for her tour.

For close to an hour, she and her husband wandered between the grave markers. As they

meandered, they read the stories of those buried beneath the rocky ground and enjoyed their time exploring Boothill.

Then, without warning, Linda was hit by another wave of dizziness. This one was even more powerful than the wave she'd felt walking into the visitor's center. Instantly, Linda felt weak and began to have a hard time breathing. She tried to keep walking but could barely stay on her feet.

As she tried to catch her breath, she stopped for a moment and noticed the name on the grave marker she was standing next to. It said China Mary.

In that moment, she felt the world swirl around her. Her chest suddenly felt very tight, as if someone was standing on top of her. She gasped for air, unable to breathe. She was being overwhelmed by a supernatural presence. She needed to get out of there!

Slowly, Linda made her way back to her car. With every step she took away from China Mary's grave, her symptoms decreased. By the time she reached the parking lot, the pain in her chest was gone completely. She was able to breathe again.

Trying to understand what had happened, Linda started to piece the clues together.

She believes the dizziness she felt was the presence of China Mary's spirit. When Linda later discovered that Mary had died of heart failure, her chest pains started to make more sense to her. Perhaps Linda was experiencing what the dead woman felt in the final moments before her life ended? And the woman she saw walking through the closed graveyard in a red dress? Linda feels certain it was the spirit of China Mary.

Is the woman in red *really* China Mary? Those who have seen the apparition sure think so. But there is probably only one way to decide for yourself, and it will require you to make your own trip out to Boothill Graveyard.

That is, if you dare!

Boothill Graveyard

A Ghostly Goodbye

For a town nicknamed "too tough to die," Tombstone sure has a lot of dead! But maybe those who made this Wild West town their home are too tough to *stay* dead? All the paranormal activity in this spookily historic hotspot sure makes it seem like that might be the case!

What do you think? Are *you* ready to pull on your boots, grab your cowboy hat, and seek out these ghostly legends? If so, I tip my hat to you. Some of those outlaws seemed plenty scary when they were alive—I cannot image how frightening they are now! Good thing the ghostly bullets of otherworldly outlaws can't hurt the living. (At least, I sure hope not.)

If you *do* decide to go looking for your own ghostly adventures, watch out! You just might get more than you bargained for. Ghosts that seem a little spooky in this book might be TERRIFYING in real life, so be sure to follow a few basic rules:

First, stick to places you are allowed to enter. (Many people do *not* welcome ghost hunters on their property.) Second, if you do get permission to seek out the spirits, make sure your ghostly adventure is a safe one. Remember to stay in groups, take notes, and always watch your back.

After all, you never know who—or WHAT— might be right behind you!

Anna Lardinois tingles the spines of Milwaukee locals and visitors through her haunted, historical walking tours known as Gothic Milwaukee. The former English teacher is an ardent collector of stories, an avid walker, and a sweet-treat enthusiast. She happily resides in a historic home in Milwaukee that, at this time, does not appear to be haunted. To learn more, visit annalardinois.com.

Check out some of the other *Spooky America* titles available now!

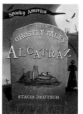

Spooky America was adapted from the creeptastic *Haunted America* series for adults. *Haunted America* explores historical haunts in cities and regions across America. Here's more from the original *Haunted Tombstone* author Cody Polston:

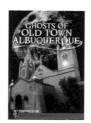
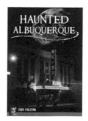